Alexandra + Joe –

I dear you know
how to throw a
party.

THE
BUBBLY BAR

I hope these cocktails
add some sparkle to
your next soirée.

Cheers, –
Nava

THE BUBBLY BAR

CHAMPAGNE AND SPARKLING WINE COCKTAILS
FOR EVERY OCCASION

Maria C. Hunt

CLARKSON POTTER/PUBLISHERS
NEW YORK

Copyright © 2009 BY MARIA C. HUNT
Photographs copyright © 2009 BY PAUL BODY

Published in the United States by
CLARKSON POTTER/PUBLISHERS,
an imprint of the
CROWN PUBLISHING GROUP,
a division of
RANDOM HOUSE, INC., NEW YORK.
www.crownpublishing.com
www.clarksonpotter.com

CLARKSON POTTER is a trademark and POTTER with
colophon is a registered trademark of Random House, Inc.

Library of Congress Cataloging-in-Publication Data
Hunt, Maria C.
The bubbly bar / Maria C. Hunt. — 1st ed.
p. cm.
1. Cocktails. 2. Sparkling wines.
3. Champagne (Wine). I. Title.
TX951.H768 2009
641.8'74—dc22 2008051643

ISBN 978-0-307-40647-7

Printed in China

Design by JENNIFER K. BEAL DAVIS

10 9 8 7 6 5 4 3 2 1

First Edition

CONTENTS

INTRODUCTION

I'VE SIPPED FAR TOO MANY GLASSES OF
BUBBLY TO RECALL THE VERY FIRST ONE,
BUT I KNOW MY EYES WERE OPENED
TO THE BEAUTY AND VERSATILITY OF
CHAMPAGNE AND SPARKLING WINES WHILE
TRAVELING IN EUROPE FOR THE FIRST TIME.
There was a casual, relaxed ease to the way the
locals began a seafood dinner in Saint-Jean-de-Luz
in the Basque Country with their own sparkling
wine called txakoli or the way Italians went out for
a meal of San Daniele prosciutto and prosecco, the
sparkling wine from the Veneto.

The most breathtaking, though, was an all-champagne luncheon at Trianon, Moët et Chandon's historic guest home in Épernay, France, where we drank a different style of champagne with quail, foie gras, and even chocolate mousse. Ever since, I've been a bubbly girl.

Americans have traditionally celebrated with champagne, but, like Europeans, we've begun to realize that a glass of bubbly has a way of making an everyday event extraordinary. The next time you have friends over, pull out a bottle and pop the cork. Your guests will think, "For me? You shouldn't have." The thrilling bubbles and luxurious taste of champagne and sparkling wine have the power to lift our spirits, making a Tuesday-night dinner for two into a memorable celebration.

While we tend to call any wine with bubbles "champagne," only sparkling wine from the Champagne region east of Paris can rightly be called by that name. Champagne is made by a special process called *méthode champenoise,* in which wines made from chardonnay, pinot noir, or pinot meunier grapes are blended together and fermented twice, the second time in the bottle, giving the wine its distinctive tiny bubbles. All other wines with bubbles—whether from other parts of France or from Italy or the United States—are called sparkling wine. No matter where they're from, though, all wines with bubbles have this special magic.

Cheers!

COCKTAILS 101

THE KEYS TO MAKING A GOOD COCKTAIL
ARE A WELL-STOCKED BAR, A FEW HANDY
TOOLS, AND CONFIDENCE!

The tastiest cocktails balance sweetness,
tartness, and the bite of alcohol, and the natural
effervescence in sparkling wine and champagne
adds an extra layer of complexity and freshness
to this mix. The recipes in this book were created
with particular flavor notes in mind, but the best
mixologists experiment and modify their drinks to
suit their taste, and I encourage you to do the same.

Essential Ingredients

THE BUBBLY

Your cocktails are only as good as the ingredients you put in them, but that doesn't mean you should mix a $200 bottle of Dom Pérignon with orange juice to make Mimosas. In fact, I prefer to make my bubbly cocktails with sparkling wine rather than champagne, which tends to be pricier. While the classic cocktails often feature champagne, all of the recipes in this book can be made with good-quality sparkling wines that cost $16 or less. You'll find a list of affordable sparkling wines in Recommended Wines by Price (page 110) in the back of the book.

As for the Dom, an amazingly balanced and nuanced blend of nearly a hundred wines, I recommend sipping it as the wine maker intended: well-chilled and by itself!

Keep It Cool It's important to chill sparkling wine sufficiently before you uncork it. A bottle of champagne has the same force inside it as a truck tire, and opening a warm bottle of sparkling wine or champagne unleashes that force with reckless abandon. If you ever had a cork fly off wildly, chances are the bottle wasn't well chilled.

The best way to chill a bottle is to place it an ice bucket filled with a mixture of half ice and half cold water for thirty minutes. If you don't have a champagne bucket, you can let the bottle rest in the refrigerator for about an hour. The freezer can also be used if you're in a hurry, but be sure to remove the bottle in thirty minutes. A bottle of wine will explode if it freezes.

Opening the Bottle Once your bubbly is cold, opening the bottle is easy. All you need is a napkin or kitchen towel handy. Remove the top part of the foil that covers the cork. Place the palm of one hand over the top of the cork; with the other hand untwist the metal cage around the cork. Loosen the cage and take it off, quickly replacing the hand that was holding the cork down. Now place the napkin or towel over the cork. Keep holding the cork firmly with one hand, then pick up the bottle and gently twist it, moving it away from the cork. The cork should come out easily, with a sigh rather than a pop.

RIPE FRUIT

The best flavors are found in ripe, juicy fruit that's in season where you live. We can go to the grocery store and find strawberries year round, but a berry that was tough enough to travel thousands of miles won't taste as good as one grown near you.

With berries and stone fruit such as peaches, plums, and apricots, use your nose to tell you what's ripe; if it doesn't smell like a raspberry or a peach, then it's not going to taste like much either.

When I'm dying for the flavor of a fruit that's not in season, I prefer using quick-frozen fruit or a naturally flavored syrup. I especially like the fruit syrups made by Torani; they capture the natural aromas and balanced flavors in more than sixty fruit flavors.

The Right Stuff: Equipment

JIGGER

This cocktail measuring cup will help you create balanced cocktails that taste the same every time. A jigger usually has a one-ounce shot compartment on one end and one-and-a-half- or two-ounce measure on the other. A set of good measuring spoons can also stand in; two tablespoons equal a one-ounce shot.

COCKTAIL SHAKER AND STRAINER

Just about everyone has one of those attractive shiny cocktail shakers with the little metal top; the problem with these shakers is that condensation gets trapped inside, making removal of the lid a real struggle. To avoid this, use an old-fashioned Boston shaker, which is basically a tempered pint glass and metal mixing cup. The Boston shaker works in tandem with a Hawthorn strainer, which is a silver paddle with metal loops around the edge. Hold the strainer across the surface of the shaker when pouring drinks to keep the ice, lemon seeds, and whatnot from falling into the glass. If you don't have a Boston shaker on hand, you can substitute a pint glass and the metal cup from a fancy cocktail shaker.

CITRUS ZESTER

You'll want one of these to create spirals and little shavings of lemon, orange, and lime rind. Get the sharpest one you can find. A vegetable peeler can also be used to cut a wide swath (about the size of a large postage stamp) of zest.

MUDDLER

In the age of the Mojito, everyone should have one of these wooden or plastic tools that are great for mashing herbs and fruit to release their juices and oils. A large wooden spoon can stand in, though it does not muddle nearly as well.

TEA STRAINER

The fine mesh is perfect for keeping lemon pulp, strawberry seeds, and other bits of fruit out of your cocktail.

FUNNEL

This is useful for directing strained juice into a glass or for making sure you don't mar a frosted rim.

LONG-HANDLED BAR SPOON

A long spoon allows you to mix drinks in tall glasses or flutes, and to properly mix in syrups, which tend to pool at the bottom of a glass. The spoon is also used to float ingredients into a cocktail.

COCKTAIL PICKS

These aren't essential, but it's fun to add creative garnishes to your drinks. Drinks are best garnished with fruits or herbs that are used as ingredients in the cocktail.

THE CLASSICS

COCKTAIL TRENDS MAY COME AND GO,

BUT THE COCKTAILS IN THIS CHAPTER

ARE AS POPULAR TODAY AS THEY WERE

WHEN COLE PORTER, MAE WEST, AND

CARY GRANT SIPPED THEM.

It's always a good idea to have a basic repertoire

of crowd-pleasing, time-tested favorites. You'll find

those recipes here along with recipes that build

upon the classic flavor combinations found in

cocktails such as the Negroni, which gets a new life

with the addition of a crisp sparkling Moscato d'Asti.

I always say, everything tastes better with bubbly!

Champagne Cocktail

This is the granddaddy of all champagne cocktails, dating back to the mid-1800s. It's easy to see why this classic has remained popular: it has a bracing bittersweet quality that makes it impossible to stop at just one sip.

3 to 4   drops Angostura bitters (see Resources, page 111)

1   sugar cube

6   ounces brut champagne

Lemon twist, for garnish

Sprinkle the drops of bitters on the sugar cube. Drop into the bottom of a champagne flute. Top with chilled champagne. Garnish with the lemon twist.

MAKES 1 COCKTAIL

VARIATION

Substitute orange bitters or peach bitters for the Angostura bitters (see Resources, page 111).

French 75

Named for a French 75-millimeter artillery gun that was especially smooth and powerful, this gin and champagne cocktail was created by American army officers during World War One. The brandy-soaked cherry adds a subtle fruity note to this traditional cocktail.

1   ounce gin

½   ounce Homemade Sour Mix (page 96)

4 to 5   ounces brut champagne

1   brandy-soaked cherry, for garnish (see Resources, page 111)

Add the gin and sour mix to a cocktail shaker filled with ice. Shake until well chilled, about 20 times (the outside of the shaker will become frosty). Strain into a champagne flute. Fill with champagne. Garnish with the cherry in the glass.

MAKES 1 COCKTAIL

WHAT ARE BITTERS?

Bitters, made from alcohol that is flavored with bitter herbs, citrus, and other plants, add a note of complexity to cocktails. The most famous are the Angostura Aromatic Bitters, which are named after the town in Venezuela where they were first created in 1824. A doctor with Simón Bolívar's army created them as a way to improve soldiers' appetites. Bitters have had a resurgence in popularity, and bartenders that specialize in old-fashioned cocktails often use Peychaud's Bitters from New Orleans or make their own flavored bitters from scratch. A few drops of bitters in club soda also helps settle an upset stomach.

Bellini

This simple mix of white peach nectar and prosecco is a timeless drink that originated at Harry's Bar in Venice, Italy. It's named for an Italian Renaissance painter who created peachy hues.

- 1 small ripe white peach, sliced for 2 ounces puree
- 5 ounces prosecco
- 1 slice of white peach, with skin, for garnish (see Note)

In a blender, puree the peach, adding a splash of prosecco, if needed, to liquefy the peach. Add 2 ounces of the peach puree to a tall glass or flute. Top with prosecco. Garnish with the peach slice.

MAKES 1 COCKTAIL

NOTE Use a small flower-shaped cookie cutter to create a little flower out of peach to garnish the cocktail. A tiny sprig of mint makes a leaf.

VARIATION

To make the cocktail called a Rossini, substitute 2 ounces fresh strawberry juice, strained of seeds, for the peach puree. Garnish with a small strawberry on a cocktail pick.

Kir Royale

This traditional French cocktail, made with black-currant liqueur, honors former Dijon mayor Félix Kir, a heroic figure in the French Resistance. Be sure to include the lemon twist; its bitter oil adds a note of complexity that really makes the flavors sing.

- ½ ounce crème de cassis
- 5 to 6 ounces brut champagne
- Lemon twist, for garnish

Add the crème de cassis to a champagne flute. Top with the champagne and garnish with the lemon twist.

MAKES 1 COCKTAIL

CHEERS IN . . . ITALY

Cin cin (chin-chin): a reference to the clinking sound glasses make.

Champagne Julep

The recipe for this refreshing cocktail was revealed in *The Ideal Bartender,* written by African American bartender Tom Bullock in 1917. Bullock worked at the St. Louis Country Club in the early 1900s and became famous for this signature drink.

8 fresh mint leaves

2 teaspoons sugar

1 ounce brandy

4 ounces champagne

Sprig of fresh mint, for garnish

Bruise the mint leaves by rolling them between your fingers. Add the sugar, bruised mint leaves, and brandy to a rocks glass. Stir to dissolve the sugar. Fill the glass three-quarters full with crushed ice. Pour on the champagne. Garnish with a sprig of mint.

MAKES 1 COCKTAIL

CHEERS IN . . . ISRAEL

La Chaim (La KAIM): To life!

Killing Me Softly

In 1933, Ernest Hemingway created an absinthe and champagne drink called Death in the Afternoon. Absinthe—aka the Green Fairy—is legal again in the United States after having shed its ninety-year bad rap as a wildly addictive drink. Even so, Hemingway's recipe is potent, so here's a subtler way to experience the spirit's anise flavor.

1 cube sugar

1 teaspoon absinthe

½ ounce St-Germain elderflower liqueur

4 ounces champagne

1 thin slice of lemon

Add the sugar cube to a martini glass. Chill the absinthe and St-Germain in a cocktail shaker filled with ice. Strain into the martini glass. Top with the champagne. Lightly squeeze the lemon slice and float it on top of the cocktail.

MAKES 1 COCKTAIL

Naughty Negroni

Legend says that this beautiful sunset-colored cocktail was created in Florence, Italy, in the 1920s. It was named after Count Camillo Negroni, who always ordered a combination of Campari, sweet vermouth, and gin. This version is lighter thanks to the addition of the sparkling wine Moscato d'Asti.

　1　ounce Campari
　1　ounce sweet vermouth
　½　ounce gin
　4　ounces Moscato d'Asti sparkling wine
　　　Long spiral of orange peel, for garnish

Add the Campari, vermouth, and gin to a cocktail shaker filled with ice. Shake until well chilled. Pour into a champagne flute. Top off with the Moscato. Garnish with the orange peel.

MAKES 1 COCKTAIL

Crushed Velvet

The dry, rich, and lightly tannic qualities of sparkling shiraz are reminiscent of a Guinness stout and inspired me to create an all-wine version of the classic Black Velvet—a champagne and Guinness blend created in 1861 to commemorate the death of Queen Victoria's consort, Prince Albert.

　3　ounces sparkling shiraz
　3　ounces brut sparkling wine
　　　Lemon twist, for garnish

Add the sparkling shiraz and brut sparkling wine to a tall pilsner-style flute. Finish with the lemon twist.

MAKES 1 COCKTAIL

CREATING FANCY CITRUS PEEL SPIRALS

Start with a firm lemon, lime, or orange for your garnish; it's impossible to zest old or mushy fruit. Although there are several types of zesters on the market, I prefer the German-made Rösle citrus zester (see Resources, page 111); it makes large, thick strips of zest as well as tiny wisps to float in your drinks. Pressing firmly, hold the zester at an angle and run it across the surface of the fruit, starting at one point and making a slow steady path around the fruit.

To create a spiral, twirl a 4- to 5-inch length of zest around a plastic drinking straw. Wrap the spiral in plastic wrap to hold it tight, then immerse the spiral in a cup of ice water. After thirty minutes, you will have a curlicue worthy of Shirley Temple.

BUBBLETINIS

I HAVE TO ADMIT, ONE OF THE BEST
THINGS ABOUT A MARTINI IS THE SWANKY
CONICAL SHAPE OF THE GLASS.
But when I order one, sometimes I find that
it's difficult to drink such a big dose of spirits.
Bubbletinis are like martinis-lite, cocktails with a
healthy kick but lightened with a splash of bubbly.
Whether it's the mouthwatering apricot and gin
in the Apricot's Blush or the autumnal Big Apple,
you'll enjoy the sophisticated combinations of
flavors in these cocktails. Since these Bubbletinis
deliver clean and direct flavors, they're perfect for
whetting the appetite before a meal.

Aperol Flip

The orangey, bittersweet Italian aperitif Aperol makes the perfect foil for mouthwatering brut champagne in this cocktail inspired by Joel Baker of Bourbon and Branch in San Francisco. The egg white gives this combination a frothy and flirtatious air.

1   ounce Aperol

    Juice of ½ lemon

½   ounce agave nectar (see Resources, page 111)

½   ounce pasteurized egg white

2   ounces brut champagne

    Wide strip of orange zest, for garnish

In a cocktail shaker filled with ice, add the Aperol, lemon juice, agave nectar, and egg white. Shake until well chilled. Pour the champagne into a martini glass. Using a strainer, pour the Aperol mixture into the glass. Pinch the orange zest to release the oil into the glass, then lay it atop the foam.

MAKES 1 COCKTAIL

CHEERS IN . . . GERMANY
Prosit (Proh-sit): Health!

Serpentine

This lovely cocktail is so named because it has a rather snakelike way of sneaking up on you, with its beguiling and fresh blend of green grapes, cucumber, and a dry, clean-tasting gin such as Bombay Sapphire. See Resources (page 111) for a source for a muddler.

7   green grapes

6   thin slices of cucumber

    Juice of ½ lime

    Splash of Homemade Sour Mix (page 96)

1½   ounces dry gin

5 to 6   ounces prosecco

In a cocktail shaker, muddle 5 of the grapes and 5 of the cucumber slices. Fill the shaker with ice and add the lime juice, sour mix, and gin. Shake until well chilled. Strain into a martini glass. Top off with the prosecco. Sandwich the remaining cucumber slice between the remaining 2 grapes on a cocktail pick for a garnish.

MAKES 1 COCKTAIL

The Stiletto

This potent cognac and orange libation makes a sharp statement, just like a pair of Manolo Blahniks. This deep-golden cocktail was inspired by the classic French Crème d'Armagnac and champagne cocktail called Pousse Rapier, which means the "thrust of the sword."

½ ounce Grand Marnier

½ to 1 ounce cognac

4 ounces brut champagne

3 drops Angostura bitters (see Resources, page 111)

Spiral of orange zest, for garnish

Pour the Grand Marnier and cognac into a champagne flute. Top with the champagne. Add the bitters. Garnish with the zest.

MAKES 1 COCKTAIL

SHAKE IT

Pouring a drink out of a cocktail shaker seems easy, but there's a trick to getting the perfect blend into the glass: pour quickly with the shaker nearly inverted over the glass.

Fill the cocktail shaker three-quarters full of ice, and use fresh ice between cocktails. Shake it vigorously twenty times, or until your hands feel frosty. Make sure the lid is on tightly or you'll be wearing your cocktail.

Apricot's Blush

The delicate combination of bittersweet apricot brandy, aromatic gin, and champagne gives this cocktail a distinctive and slightly spicy flavor. The subtle blush of the brut rosé makes this sexy cocktail look like a ripe apricot.

½ ounce apricot brandy

½ ounce gin

¼ ounce orange bitters (see Resources, page 111)

Juice of ½ lemon

½ teaspoon confectioners' sugar

4 to 5 ounces brut rosé champagne

1 slice of fresh apricot, dusted in sugar, for garnish

Pour the brandy, gin, bitters, lemon juice, and confectioners' sugar into a cocktail shaker filled with ice. Shake until well chilled. Strain into a champagne flute. Top off with the champagne. Garnish with the slice of sugared apricot on a long bamboo skewer.

MAKES 1 COCKTAIL

Big Apple

I would never have paired the hazelnut liqueur Frangelico with sparkling wine had I not tasted the autumn seasonal sparkler at the Loews Coronado Bay Resort in California. In this adaptation, the nutty flavor, combined with the apple brandy Calvados and a hint of freshly grated nutmeg, perfectly captures the essence of autumn. The resort uses Domaine Carneros Brut in their version of this cocktail.

½ ounce Calvados

½ ounce Frangelico

5 to 6 ounces brut sparkling wine

1 very thin crosswise slice of apple

3 fresh grates of nutmeg

Add the Calvados and Frangelico to a martini glass. Top it off with the brut sparkling wine. Garnish with the apple slice, top with the grated nutmeg, and serve.

NOTE If you have a mandoline, use it to make paper-thin crosswise slices of 1 small apple.

MAKES 1 COCKTAIL

Belle de Jour

This homage to the iconic French actress Catherine Deneuve—known for playing coolly beautiful blondes—was inspired by a cocktail created by Jacqueline Patterson in San Francisco. It's smooth and lightly sweet, and the addition of the aperitif Lillet Blonde makes it 100 percent French.

½ ounce Grey Goose La Poire vodka

½ ounce white elderflower syrup (see Resources, page 111) or St-Germain elderflower liqueur

1 ounce Lillet Blonde

3 to 4 ounces brut rosé champagne

1 slice of star fruit (carambola), for garnish (see Resources, page 111)

Add the vodka, elderflower syrup, and Lillet to a cocktail shaker filled with ice. Shake until well chilled. Strain into a martini glass. Slowly pour in the champagne; it will create a two-tone effect. Cut a slit in one point of the star fruit and slip it onto the rim of the glass.

MAKES 1 COCKTAIL

FRUITFUL FIZZ

THE DUKE OF EDINBURGH ONCE OBSERVED
THAT THE COMBINATION OF CHAMPAGNE
AND ORANGE JUICE IS AN INSPIRED ONE:
"The orange improves the taste of the champagne.
The champagne definitely improves the orange."
When my favorite fruits come into season throughout
the year, I cherish their flavors as long as I can. Every
spring I fall in love with strawberries; in summertime,
I adore peaches and plums; and in autumn it's
tangerines and pomegranates. The cocktails in this
chapter make it possible to experience these seasonal
flavors in an effervescent liquid form.

Lychee Love

The seductive flavor of lychee fruit adds an elusive elegance to this exotic sparkling sake, ginger, and lemongrass cocktail. It's extra good made with fresh lychees, which are in season from late spring through mid-summer, or with a good white rum.

- 2 ounces lychee juice
- 1 ounce coconut water
- ½ ounce Lemongrass-Ginger Syrup (page 96)
- Juice of ¼ lime or one Key lime
- 1 ounce Hangar One kaffir lime vodka
- 3 ounces Zipang sparkling sake (see Resources, page 111), chilled
- 1 lychee fruit or lychee gummy candy, for garnish (see Resources, page 111)

Add the lychee juice, coconut water, lemongrass-ginger syrup, lime juice, and vodka to a cocktail shaker filled with ice and shake until well chilled. Strain into a martini glass. Top off with the sparkling sake. Garnish with a lychee fruit or lychee gummy candy on a bamboo cocktail skewer.

MAKES 1 COCKTAIL

Cantaloupe Crush

Celebrate the heat of summer with this lush cocktail that blends the sweetly smooth taste of Bärenjäger, a honey liqueur from Germany, with the lush flavor of a ripe cantaloupe.

- ½ cup cantaloupe (to make 1½ ounces cantaloupe juice)
- 1 ounce Bärenjäger honey liqueur
- 1 ounce Earl Grey tea, lightly steeped and chilled
- Juice of ¼ lemon
- 3 ounces dry sparkling wine

In a blender, puree the cantaloupe and strain the juice through a tea strainer. Pour 1½ ounces of the cantaloupe juice into a cocktail shaker filled with ice, along with the Bärenjäger, tea, and lemon juice. Shake until well chilled. Strain into a short champagne flute. Top with the sparkling wine.

MAKES 1 COCKTAIL

> ### CHEERS IN . . . JAPAN
> *Kampai* (kahm-PIE): "Dry cup" as in "bottoms up!"

Tiziano

Freshly squeezed grape juice has a delicious taste that can't be found in a bottle. Legendary restaurateur Harry Cipriani is said to have created this cocktail, but I discovered it at Tra Vigne restaurant in St. Helena, California, where it's described as a favorite harvest-time tipple.

7 to 10 red grapes (to make 1½ ounces fresh-pressed red grape juice)

4 to 5 ounces prosecco

1 red grape, for garnish

1 green grape, for garnish

Puree the grapes in a blender. Strain the puree through a sieve into a champagne flute. Discard the grape pulp. Top with the prosecco. Garnish with the red and green grapes threaded on a long bamboo skewer.

MAKES 1 COCKTAIL

VARIATION

This cocktail takes on a whole different flavor when made with green grapes or an aromatic variety such as muscats or concords.

Tangerine Dream

While tangerine and vanilla recall the flavors of a Dreamsicle, thyme syrup adds a sophisticated note to this cocktail made with prosecco, an Italian sparkling wine.

Juice of 1 small tangerine (2 ounces)

1 ounce Vanilla-Infused Soju (page 98)

½ ounce Thyme Syrup (page 97)

4 to 5 ounces prosecco

One sprig of fresh thyme, for garnish

Add the tangerine juice, soju, and thyme syrup to a cocktail shaker filled with ice. Shake until well chilled. Strain into a champagne flute. Top off with the prosecco. Garnish with the thyme.

MAKES 1 COCKTAIL

SPIRITED SOJU

Korean soju is a clear, flavorless spirit distilled from rice, barley, or sweet potatoes that's becoming popular in American bars and restaurants. Soju is a perfect substitute for vodka in Bloody Marys and for tequila in margaritas. Han Soju, one of the leading companies, offers two sojus, an 80-proof version and a 48-proof version called Pure. I prefer the Pure for mixing with sparkling wine and champagne; either one can be easily infused.

Pattaya

I discovered this luscious cocktail, named after a beach in Thailand, at Spice Market in New York City. If you float the blackberry liqueur just right you'll see a sunset in your glass. An organic dendrobium orchid is another pretty garnish.

½ ounce Torani passion fruit syrup (see Resources, page 111)

5 ounces brut champagne, chilled

½ ounce blackberry liqueur

1 blackberry, for garnish

3- to 4-inch strip of lemon zest, for garnish

Pour the passion fruit syrup into a champagne flute. Add the champagne. Float the blackberry liqueur by slowly pouring it over the back of a teaspoon to create a layered effect. Garnish with a blackberry wrapped with lemon zest.

MAKES 1 COCKTAIL

Lava Lamp

This sweet-tart pomegranate cocktail looks as good as it tastes. The bubbles in the sparkling wine make the pomegranate seeds rise and fall in the glass, giving this drink the appearance of a retro lava lamp. A flute with a long hollow stem shows off this effect best.

1 ounce Pama pomegranate liqueur or 3 tablespoons pomegranate juice

5 ounces brut sparkling wine

3 pomegranate seeds

Add the pomegranate liqueur or pomegranate juice to a champagne flute. Fill the glass with sparkling wine. Drop in the pomegranate seeds.

MAKES 1 COCKTAIL

FLOATING LIQUEURS

Creating a layered drink, such as the B-52 shot of Kahlúa, Bailey's, and Grand Marnier, seems mysterious, but actually it's quite simple. The technique called "floating" was perfected in the late 1800s in New Orleans, when every bartender could make a Pousse Café—a rainbow drink with four to six perfect stripes of liqueur. The sugary, heavier mixers such as grenadine or crème de cassis are carefully added to the glass. Then lighter spirits with more alcohol, such as maraschino or brandy, are poured over the back of a spoon, causing them to rest on top of the previous layer. For the Pattaya, add the passion fruit syrup and brut to the glass. Rest an upturned bar spoon against the inside of the glass and slowly pour the crème de cassis across the back of the spoon. The crème de cassis will pool at the bottom in a purplish layer. Once you've mastered this, try inventing your own layered drinks.

Framboise Apricot Punch

My friend Kalisa makes a wickedly delicious holiday punch each year that hits the perfect balance between sweet, tart, and potent with its combination of cognac, apricot brandy, and raspberry eau-de-vie—known as framboise. Start this punch the day before you plan to serve it.

1 cup orange juice

½ cup water

1 cup pomegranate seeds, divided

¾ cup framboise (raspberry eau-de-vie)

½ cup VSOP cognac

¼ cup apricot brandy

1 orange, thinly sliced

1 lemon, thinly sliced

½ cup sugar

½ cup Homemade Sour Mix (page 96)

2 bottles brut sparkling wine

Combine the orange juice, water, and ½ cup of the pomegranate seeds in a small ring mold or a small square plastic container with a lid. Freeze for 24 hours. Combine the framboise, cognac, apricot brandy, orange and lemon slices, and sugar in a plastic container. Let the fruit soak in the liquor overnight.

The day you plan to serve the punch, pour the sour mix and 2 bottles of sparkling wine into a large punch bowl. Add the liquor-soaked fruit, syrup, and the remaining ½ cup of pomegranate seeds. Crown the punch with the orange and pomegranate ice mold, which will keep the punch cold.

MAKES 12 SERVINGS (ENOUGH FOR 6 PEOPLE)

> ## CHEERS IN . . . FRANCE
> *A santé* (ah san-tay): To health!

ROSE-COLORED GLASSES

PERHAPS I'M AN OPTIMIST, BUT I FIND
SOMETHING EXCEPTIONALLY CHEERFUL
ABOUT A PINK BUBBLY DRINK.

Sadly, many people mistake rosé champagnes
and sparkling wines as being unsophisticated and
sweet. Actually, many rosés are dry, crisp wines
that hint of red fruit such as raspberries and plums.
The rosé version of many champagnes costs far
more than the pale gold version. Domaine Chandon
and Korbel in California, Blason de Bourgogne
from France, and Jacob's Creek from Australia all
make fine affordable, dry rosés that would
be perfect in a cocktail.

Ruby Red Sangria

This fragrant sangria, created by Tom Mastricola, a great bartender who lives in San Diego, is made with the sweet, red sparkling wine Brachetto d'Acqui. The cognac adds an extra layer of depth and flavor.

2   raspberries

2   blueberries

2   strawberries

1   slice of orange

1   slice of lemon

1   ounce Landy cognac

½   ounce crème de cassis

½   ounce Homemade Sour Mix (page 96)
   Splash of fresh orange juice

2 to 3   ounces Rosa Regale Brachetto d'Acqui (see Resources, page 111)

Add the berries to a cocktail shaker and muddle them to a juicy pulp. Add the orange and lemon slices. Add the cognac, crème de cassis, sour mix, and orange juice and stir well to combine. Pour into a rocks glass, tall drinking glass, or narrow collins glass. Fill the glass with crushed ice. Top off with the Brachetto.

MAKES 1 COCKTAIL

Sugar Plum

Sweet plum wine lends this drink its fragrance and flavor, while sparkling sake adds a balancing crispness. Any ripe summer plum can be used, but Santa Rosas are my favorite.

2   ounces plum wine

1   ounce soju (see page 39)
   Splash of grenadine
   Juice of ¼ lime

2   drops Angostura bitters

3   slices ripe, fresh red or purple plum

4   ounces sparkling sake (see Resources, page 111)

Add the plum wine, soju, grenadine, lime juice, and bitters to a tall collins glass and stir. Fill the glass one-third full with ice and add a slice of plum. Continue alternating layers of ice with the plum slices until the glass is three-quarters full. Fill the glass with the sparkling sake. Stir lightly and serve.

MAKES 1 COCKTAIL

CHEERS IN . . . CHINA (MANDARIN)
Gan Bei (gon-bay): Dry your cup!

Crown Princess

Plump, fragrant blueberries and ripe pineapple are essential to this cocktail. The refreshing combination of berries, pineapple, and the raspberry liqueur Chambord is balanced by the aromatic and smooth botanical notes in the gin.

½ cup blueberries, enough for 1 ounce blueberry juice, plus 3 whole blueberries, for garnish

1 ounce fresh pineapple juice

½ ounce Chambord

½ ounce dry gin

4 ounces brut rosé sparkling wine

1 raspberry, for garnish

Puree the blueberries in a blender and strain the juice through a tea strainer. Add the juice to a tall collins glass, along with the pineapple juice, Chambord, and gin. Fill the glass with crushed ice. Top with the brut rosé. To garnish, thread the 3 blueberries onto a long bamboo skewer; add the raspberry at the top.

MAKES 1 COCKTAIL

Watermelon Sour

This gorgeous watermelon-pink confection was inspired by a fantastic cocktail created by Tony Abou-Ganim of Bar Milano in New York City, a modern mixologist who makes cocktails with the same attention to flavor that chefs bring to fine cuisine. This cocktail is so well balanced, it tastes like a lovely watermelon lemonade.

½ cup watermelon, enough for 2 ounces watermelon juice

¼ ounce Homemade Sour Mix (page 96)

½ ounce Alizé Red Passion

1 ounce delicate gin

3 ounces brut rosé sparkling wine

2 small melon balls, for garnish

1 slice of lime, for garnish

Puree the watermelon in a blender and strain through a tea strainer. Add 2 ounces of the watermelon juice, the sour mix, Alizé, and gin to a cocktail shaker filled with ice. Shake until well chilled. Strain into a martini glass. Top off with the brut rosé. Garnish with the melon balls and lime slice on a cocktail pick.

MAKES 1 COCKTAIL

Sour Cherry

Sweet-tart dried cherries from Michigan are one of my favorite things in the world; I can eat them by the handful. When I discovered sour cherry syrup at a Middle Eastern grocery in my neighborhood, I created a cocktail to showcase their intense flavor.

½ ounce Luxardo maraschino liqueur

½ ounce sour cherry syrup (see Resources, page 111)

½ ounce brandy

2 drops Angostura bitters

Juice of ¼ lemon

3 ounces brut champagne

2 brandy-soaked cherries, for garnish (see Resources, page 111)

Add the maraschino liqueur, cherry syrup, brandy, bitters, and lemon juice to a cocktail shaker filled with ice. Shake until well chilled. Strain into a champagne flute. Top off with the champagne. Garnish by dropping the cherries in the glass.

MAKES 1 COCKTAIL

CHEERS IN . . . POLAND
Na zdrowie (nas drove-yah): To your health!

Pink Cream Soda

Bourbon and Branch is a modern speakeasy in San Francisco. Patrons must make a reservation online and then give a password at the door before being served some serious cocktails. The bar's former manager Todd Smith won a cocktail contest I was judging with this sublime creation using grapefruit, vanilla, and rosé champagne.

2 grapefruit segments

½ ounce Torani pink grapefruit syrup (see Resources, page 111)

1 ounce grapefruit juice

1 ounce guava nectar

1 ounce Vanilla-Infused Soju (page 98)

2 ounces brut rosé sparkling wine or champagne

Bendy straw (optional)

Sprig of fresh mint, for garnish

Fill a collins glass one-third full with crushed ice; drop in a grapefruit segment. Fill another third with ice and add the other grapefruit segment; top off with more ice. In a cocktail shaker filled with ice, add the pink grapefruit syrup, grapefruit juice, guava nectar, and soju. Shake until well chilled. Pour into the prepared glass. Top off with the brut rosé and garnish with the bendy straw and mint, if using.

MAKES 1 COCKTAIL

LATIN LIBATIONS

THE RIPE, LUSCIOUS FLAVORS OF LATIN
AMERICA CAN BE FOUND IN MANY OF
OUR FAVORITE COCKTAILS, WHETHER
the bright lime of a margarita, or the sweet
creaminess of pineapple and coconut in a Piña
Colada. I've called upon Latin flavors such as
mango, hibiscus, and tamarind to create new
classics with a tropical twist. For these vibrant,
sparkling cocktails, I especially like using cava, the
sparkling wine made from native grapes in Spain
by the same careful winemaking techniques
that are used to make champagne.

Hibiscus Sipper

This spicy crowd pleaser combines aromatic kaffir lime with the bright flavor of the traditional jamaica (ha-MY-kuh), a deep-red brew of dried hibiscus flowers and warm spices that's served at many taco shops. Hibiscus or jamaica tea can be found in the Latin food section of most grocery stores, or see Resources, page 111.

     2   ounces spiced hibiscus tea, chilled (recipe follows)
     ¾   ounce Hangar One kaffir lime vodka
     1   ounce Lemongrass-Ginger Syrup (page 96)
2 to 3   ounces brut cava
     1   slice of Key lime, for garnish
     6   cloves, for garnish
         Ground cinnamon, for garnish

Add the cold tea, vodka, and lemongrass-ginger syrup to a cocktail shaker filled with ice. Shake until well chilled. Strain into a tall collins glass filled with ice cubes. Top off with the sparkling wine. Using a bamboo skewer, poke six holes around the edge of the lime. Fill the holes with the cloves. Garnish with the slice of Key lime and a sprinkle of cinnamon.

MAKES 1 COCKTAIL

Spiced Hibiscus Tea

2 bags hibiscus tea
½ cinnamon stick
3 whole cloves
2 star anise

Place the tea bag, cinnamon, cloves, and star anise in a tempered-glass mixing cup. Bring ½ cup water to a boil and pour over the tea bag and spices. Let steep for 10 minutes. Cool completely before adding to a cocktail.

> **CHEERS IN . . . BRAZIL**
> *Saude* (sow-oo-juh): To your health!

> **CHEERS IN . . . MEXICO**
> *Salud* (sa-LOOD): To your health!

Sangria Blanca

There's something elegant about white sangria made by combining a crisp cava, a fragrant white rum made from fresh sugarcane juice, and tart white cranberry juice. This recipe tastes best when made the night before serving, but it can also be whipped up on short notice. Serve over ice on a warm day.

- 4 ounces fragrant white rum, such as 10 Cane
- 3 ounces Cointreau
- ½ ounce Angostura bitters
- ½ ounce orange bitters (see Resources, page 111)
- 3 ounces Homemade Sour Mix (page 96)
- 1 cup green seedless grapes, halved
- 2 ripe peaches or nectarines, thinly sliced
- 1 star fruit (carambola), sliced (see Resources, page 111)
- 2 cups white cranberry juice
- 1 bottle cava
- 8 leaves of fresh mint, chopped

Combine the rum, Cointreau, bitters, and sour mix in a small mixing cup. Add the grapes, peaches, and star fruit. Soak the fruit overnight or for at least 2 hours.

When ready to assemble, add the soaked fruit to a large pitcher or punch bowl. Add the white cranberry juice, cava, and mint. Give it a good stir and then serve.

MAKES 8 SERVINGS

Sparkling Pisco Sour

Peru and Chile both claim to have created the classic Pisco Sour, which is made with the potent grape brandy called Pisco. The egg whites give the drink a perfect frothy halo that floats above the zesty lime confection.

- 1 ounce Pisco
- 1 ounce Homemade Sour Mix (page 96)
- ½ teaspoon pasteurized egg whites
- 3 drops Angostura bitters
- 2 ounces brut sparkling wine
- 1 thin slice of lime, for garnish
- 1 green or red grape, for garnish

Add the Pisco, sour mix, egg whites, and bitters to a cocktail shaker filled with ice. Shake until well chilled. Strain into a champagne flute. Top off with the sparkling wine. To create a garnish, slit the lime slice three quarters of the way through, almost up to the rind. Overlap the cut ends to form a cone. Place the grape in the middle and secure the bundle with a cocktail pick.

MAKES 1 COCKTAIL

Pure Passion

Turn up the heat with the spicy bite of chile and the tangy flavor of passion fruit in this seductive potion. If passion fruit is in season, use fresh strained juice.

½ cup sugar

½ teaspoon chile powder

½ teaspoon salt

½ Key or Mexican lime

2 ounces fresh passion fruit juice or canned (see Resources, page 111)

Juice of ½ lime

½ ounce Cointreau

4 ounces brut cava

Combine the sugar, chile powder, and salt in a wide flat plastic container. Set aside.

Make a slit down the length of the Key lime and run it around the rim of a wide-mouthed glass, wetting it thoroughly. Press the rim of the glass into the chile-sugar mixture to coat the rim.

Combine the passion fruit juice, lime juice, and Cointreau in a cocktail shaker filled with ice. Shake until well chilled, and then carefully strain into the prepared glass. Top with the brut cava wine.

MAKES 1 COCKTAIL

CREATING FROSTED RIMS ON COCKTAILS

Frosting the rim of a glass adds a stylish detail and another layer of flavor to your cocktails. A sugared rim can balance a tart cocktail, a nutmeg rim can add a warm spicy note, and a peppered rim can add depth to a sweet drink.

The technique is really simple. First, you'll need to set up a sugaring station: I find that shallow round plastic deli containers work well for mixing sugars, salts, and spices, but a small plate can also work in a pinch (just make sure to thoroughly mix your spices with the salt or sugar before placing on the plate). Add about ½ cup sugar or salt and ½ teaspoon of any spice you may be using to your container, place the lid on securely, and shake. Remove the lid; flatten out the sugar or salt. Slice a Key lime or small lemon in half lengthwise and then make a shallow cut down the axis so it easily fits on the rim of the glass. Squeeze lightly as you run the fruit all the way around the rim of the glass. Press the moistened rim of the glass into the mixture. Lift the glass and set it aside for a few minutes so the rim has time to dry.

Tamarindo

Fragrant tamarind pods are prized for their sweet-and-sour brown pulp. Paired with a Martinique sugarcane rum called rhum agricole, tamarind's flavor makes this cocktail a perfectly refreshing treat, while the jalapeño adds a spicy note.

1 ounce tamarind syrup (see Note)

1 ounce good golden rum or rhum agricole, such as Rhum Clément

   Juice of ½ lime or 1 Mexican lime

½ ounce orange bitters, such as Fee Brothers

3 to 4 ounces brut cava

   Orange slice, for garnish

1 slice of jalapeño pepper (optional)

Add the tamarind syrup, rum, lime juice, and orange bitters to a cocktail shaker filled with ice. Shake until well chilled and strain into a champagne flute. Top with the cava. Garnish with the slice of orange and, if using, slice of jalapeño on a long bamboo skewer. The jalapeño can be swirled in the drink for added flavor and then discarded.

MAKES 1 COCKTAIL

NOTE Tamarind syrup is available at Latin or Middle Eastern markets.

Tisana Punch

Inspired by a fruit punch commonly served in Venezuela, this golden concoction is always appreciated. Try my version of this classic, and then feel free to vary the ingredients with the fruits and juices you might have on hand, taking care to balance the sweet and tart flavors. A good dark rum can also be substituted for the brandy.

2 cups pineapple juice

2 cups orange juice

2 cups pink grapefruit juice

1½ cups passion fruit juice

1 ripe mango, diced

1 green apple, cored and diced

   Pulp from 1 passion fruit

6 ounces brandy

2 teaspoons Angostura bitters

2 bottles cava

10 fresh shavings of nutmeg

Combine the juices and fruits in a punch bowl or large pitcher and then add the brandy and bitters. Pour in the cava. Top with the freshly grated nutmeg and serve with ice if you like.

MAKES 12 SERVINGS

BUBBLES IN BLOOM

BEYOND THE OCCASIONAL NASTURTIUM
BLOSSOM IN A SALAD, EATING
FLOWERS SEEMS EXOTIC TO SOME.
But in traveling around the world, it's not
uncommon to find the unique aromas and flavors
of roses, violets, and orange blossoms in a variety
of dishes. These delicious floral scents are amplified
by the bubbles in sparkling wine, which disperse
little bursts of fragrance into the air. When making
cocktails only use organic flowers that are free of
pesticides and chemicals; get them from an organic
grocery, a farmers' market, or your own garden.

Violet Fizz

The distinctly floral flavor of violets adds a fresh twist to the classic Ramos Gin Fizz, giving this cocktail a decadent, old-fashioned feeling. Creamy colored when it's first poured, this cocktail takes on a lovely violet hue as you sip.

- 4 ounces brut sekt or prosecco
- ½ ounce Monin violet syrup (see Resources, page 111)
- 1 ounce delicate gin, such as Martin Miller's
  Juice of ½ lemon
- ½ ounce pasteurized egg white
- 2 pieces of candied violet (see Resources, page 111), for garnish

Pour the sekt or prosecco into a martini glass. Add the violet syrup, gin, lemon juice, and egg white to a cocktail shaker filled with ice. Shake until well chilled. Strain the mixture into the martini glass. Garnish with the candied violet.

MAKES 1 COCKTAIL

Pink Jasmine

The tart flavor of pink grapefruit balances the intoxicating fragrance of jasmine and anise in this seductively simple cocktail.

- 1½ ounces chilled jasmine green tea
- ½ ounce Monin jasmine syrup (see Resources, page 111)
- 2 ounces pink grapefruit juice
- 1 teaspoon Pernod or clear anise-flavored liqueur
- 3 ounces brut sparkling wine
  Jasmine blossom, for garnish (optional)

Add the chilled tea, jasmine syrup, grapefruit juice, and Pernod or anise liqueur to a cocktail shaker filled with ice. Shake until well chilled. Strain into a champagne flute. Top with the sparkling wine. If you'd like, float a jasmine blossom on the cocktail for garnish and serve.

MAKES 1 COCKTAIL

Lavender Tea

The calming fragrance of lavender and the natural vanilla flavor of rooibus tea make this cocktail perfect for a quiet evening at home or a relaxing afternoon on the porch. It's inspired by a traditional cocktail in Alsace made with crémant d'Alsace and lemon verbena tea.

Make the lavender tea by steeping two bags in one cup of boiling water for four minutes. Let the tea cool before proceeding.

1   Key lime, sliced

    Lavender sugar (recipe follows)

3   ounces cooled lightly steeped lavender rooibus tea, such as Zhena's Gypsy Tea Red Lavender or other lavender tea (see Resources, page 111)

1   ounce Homemade Sour Mix (page 96)

3   ounces chilled brut sparkling wine

Moisten the rim of a tumbler or flute with the sliced Key lime. Press the rim of the glass into the lavender sugar, shaking off the excess.

Add the lavender tea and the sour mix to the glass, being careful not to disturb the sugared rim. Top off with the sparkling wine. Serve with ice if you prefer.

MAKES 1 COCKTAIL

VARIATION

This recipe also works well with delicately flavored linden tea, which is variously known as *tilleul* in France, *tila* in Spain, and lime flower in the United States. If substituting, omit the lavender sugar and follow the same instructions, replacing the lavender tea with linden tea. It will have an equally calming effect.

Lavender Sugar

10 dried lavender flowers (see Resources, page 111)

½ cup sugar

Crush the lavender into the sugar and combine thoroughly. Store the sugar in an airtight container in a cabinet or other room-temperature spot. It will last indefinitely.

Vintage Rose

This subtly fragrant cocktail offers a hint of vanilla from the Tuaca liqueur, and a hint of rose thanks to a tisane made from dried rose petals. Organic dried rose petals can be found in the Latin spices section of the grocery store.

- 2 ounces cooled rose tisane (recipe follows)
- 1 ounce Tuaca
- 4 ounces cava or prosecco
- 1 fresh organic rose petal or dried organic rose blossom, for garnish

Add the rose tisane and Tuaca to a champagne flute. Fill with the cava or prosecco. Garnish with the rose petal or blossom.

MAKES 1 COCKTAIL

Rose Tisane

⅛ cup dried pink rose petals (see Resources, page 111)

Steep the rose petals in ½ cup boiling water for 5 minutes. Strain the liquid and let cool before using.

Elderbubble

I first tasted this cocktail at Laurel Restaurant and Bar in San Diego, and the haunting flavor of white elderflower syrup, reminiscent of lychee fruit, quickly became a favorite.

- 1 ounce white elderflower syrup (see Resources, page 111) or St-Germain elderflower liqueur
- ½ ounce raspberry vodka
- 3 to 4 ounces brut champagne
- 2 fresh or frozen raspberries, for garnish

Add the elderflower syrup and raspberry vodka to a champagne flute. Top off with the champagne. Garnish with the raspberries.

MAKES 1 COCKTAIL

MAKING THE MAGIC LAST

There are a few myths about how to keep an open bottle of champagne bubbly. One involves sticking the handle of a metal spoon into the bottle but that really doesn't work. Don't stopper the bottle with a regular wine cork; the bubbles can and will make the cork fly off, especially if the bottle gets warm or shaken up.

My fail-safe is using a champagne stopper: a springy cap with two arms that clamp down around the lip of the bottle and hold the cork in place. Silver cylindrical stoppers are available at liquor stores and online, but I prefer the tighter fit of the more streamlined versions found at most wineries. You'll need a few sizes because the lip of each bottle is made a bit differently.

Love in the Afternoon

The piquant flavor of tangerine, combined with cooling mint and calming rosewater, makes this cocktail ideal for a relaxing, dreamy midday potion. In the movie *Le Divorce,* set in Paris, a similar combination was described as the perfect drink to sip before romance.

    2   ounces fresh tangerine juice
    1   ounce rosewater
    2   fresh mint leaves
    4   ounces dry (slightly sweet) champagne

Add the tangerine juice and rosewater to a champagne flute. Twist the mint leaves in your fingers and drop them in the glass. Fill the glass with the champagne.

MAKES 1 COCKTAIL

CHEERS IN . . . GREECE
Yassou (yah-sue): Bless you!

Cotton Candy

This bright little confection, with its delicate floral aroma, was inspired by Robert Ferrias, a bartender at the Starlight Room in San Francisco. He makes it with an orange flower–infused vodka, but it works just as well with a combination of unflavored vodka and orange flower water.

    1   ounce vodka
    3   drops orange flower water
    2   ounces freshly squeezed pink grapefruit juice
    ½   ounce cranberry juice
    ½   ounce agave nectar (see Resources, page 111)
    2   ounces brut rosé champagne or rosé sparkling wine
         1-inch wedge of grapefruit, for garnish

Combine the vodka, orange flower water, pink grapefruit juice, cranberry juice, and agave nectar in a cocktail shaker filled with ice and shake until well chilled. Strain into a champagne flute. Top with the rosé champagne or rosé sparkling wine. Garnish with the wedge of grapefruit.

MAKES 1 COCKTAIL

MIXED AND MUDDLED

WE MIGHT THINK THE WORD *MUDDLED*
REFERS TO A STATE OF CONFUSION IF NOT
FOR TWO BELOVED COCKTAILS: CUBA'S
MOJITO AND BRAZIL'S CAIPIRINHA.
Both are made using a tool called a muddler to
mash the ingredients to release their juices and oils
into the glass. Charmed by the honest flavors of
these cocktails, bartenders are creating all sorts of
drinks with fresh fruits that are mashed by hand.
Treat yourself to the kaleidoscope effect of colorful
muddled fruit and bubbly in these recipes.

Hemingway's Mojito

Writer Ernest Hemingway was said to be especially fond of these bright, minty cocktails served at La Bodeguita del Medio in Havana, Cuba, which is considered the birthplace of the Mojito. Although the cocktail is commonly made with club soda, Hemingway—clearly a man of taste—preferred his with champagne.

- 6 fresh mint leaves
  Juice of 1 lime
- 2 teaspoons light brown sugar
- 1½ ounces white rum, such as 10 Cane
- 3 ounces champagne
  Sprig of fresh mint, for garnish

In a rocks glass, add the mint leaves, lime juice, and brown sugar. Muddle to release the mint oil. Add the rum and fill the glass three-quarters full with ice. Top off with the champagne. Garnish with the mint sprig.

MAKES 1 COCKTAIL

Il Sorrentino

Like everyone from Sorrento, Italy, my friend Antonio makes homemade limoncello, a bitter-sweet lemon liqueur. Mixed with prosecco and the herb lemon balm, it's a refreshing citrusy drink.

- 4 thin slices of lemon
- 4 thin slices of lime
- 4 thin slices of tangerine
- 2 fresh lemon balm or mint leaves
- 1 ounce limoncello
- ½ ounce Homemade Sour Mix (page 96)
- 5 ounces prosecco

Add 3 of the lemon, lime, and tangerine slices and the lemon balm (or mint) to a rocks glass and muddle. Add the limoncello and sour mix and stir. Fill the glass three-quarters full with ice. Top with the prosecco. Garnish with the remaining slices of lemon, lime, and tangerine.

MAKES 1 COCKTAIL

HOW TO MUDDLE

Traditional muddlers are made of wood, but muddlers with a plastic end can be cleaned more thoroughly.

Place the ingredients you want to muddle in a heavy rocks glass or a pint mixing glass. Using a gentle rolling motion, slowly and firmly start to mash the fruit or herbs. Don't rush or get too vigorous. Soft fruits such as berries and grapes will completely lose their shape when properly muddled. Fresh herbs, fresh ginger, and citrus fruits will retain their shape but look bruised, and you'll smell their juice and oils more strongly.

Ginger Snap

The buzzy taste of ginger and the tang of lemon and lime (in the sour mix) give this cocktail a yin-yang balance that makes it both crisp and refreshing. It pairs well with an Asian meal and could easily be made with a brut sparkling wine.

  3 thin slices of peeled fresh gingerroot

  ½ ounce Homemade Sour Mix (page 96)

  1 ounce Domaine de Couton ginger liqueur

  4 ounces dry sparkling sake, such as Zipang (see Resources, page 111)

  2 slivers of candied ginger, for garnish (see Resources, page 111)

Add the ginger and sour mix to a rocks glass and muddle until the ginger is bruised and begins to smell. Strain the ginger and sour mixture into a champagne flute. Top with the ginger liqueur and sparkling sake. Garnish with the candied ginger.

MAKES 1 COCKTAIL

CHEERS IN . . . THE PHILIPPINES
Mabuhay (Ma-bu-hai): Long life!

Fraise des Bois

Black pepper syrup brings an unexpected kick to the summer-fresh taste of strawberries and basil in this delicious cocktail. Make these by the pitcher and you'll have the perfect refreshment for a hot summer day.

    3 large ripe strawberries

    3 fresh basil leaves

    1 ounce Homemade Sour Mix (page 96)

    1 ounce soju (see page 39)

4 to 5 ounces brut rosé

    ½ ounce Black Pepper Syrup (page 97)

    1 small strawberry, for garnish

Add the large strawberries and the basil to a rocks glass and muddle until the strawberries are thoroughly mashed. Add the sour mix and soju; mix with a bar spoon to combine. Fill the glass with crushed ice. Top with the brut rosé. Drizzle with the black pepper syrup. Garnish with the small strawberry.

MAKES 1 COCKTAIL

Cucumber Cooler

This pale green cocktail may be the closest a drink can come to being good for you. Agave nectar is a sweetener made from wild agave plants in Mexico, and it has a less marked effect on blood sugar than do other sweeteners.

6 thin slices of cucumber

½ ounce Rain organic vodka

Juice of ½ lime or 1 Mexican lime

¾ ounce agave nectar (see Resources, page 111)

5 ounces dry sparkling sake, such as Zipang (see Resources, page 111)

1 cube cucumber, for garnish

Muddle the cucumber slices and the vodka in a rocks glass. Add the lime juice and agave nectar, stirring to mix thoroughly. Fill glass three-quarters full with ice. Top with the sparkling sake. Garnish with the cucumber cube on a cocktail pick.

MAKES 1 COCKTAIL

TO STRAIN OR NOT TO STRAIN?

I enjoy the sweet mash of fruit and herbs in muddled fruit cocktails, but not everyone feels the same. Let the occasion be your cue. For elegant parties, strain fruits from cocktails; nobody wants seeds stuck in their teeth. Double-strain very seedy or pulpy fruits with a tea strainer. If you're entertaining in the backyard, leave the pulp in the drink for extra color and flavor.

Bubbling Blackberry Bramble

Blackberry and cucumber may sound like an unusual combination, but the rose geranium syrup, with its slightly fruity flavor, links them together in this cocktail.

12 ripe blackberries (to make 2 ounces juice)

3 thin slices of cucumber

½ ounce Rose Geranium Syrup (page 98)

Juice of ½ lime

½ ounce gin

5 ounces dry sparkling wine

1 long thin strip of cucumber, for garnish

Muddle the blackberries and cucumber slices in a cocktail shaker. Strain the juice through a tea strainer into a jigger to measure 2 ounces. Pour into a rocks glass. Add the Rose Geranium Syrup, lime juice, and gin and stir. Fill the glass three-quarters full with ice. Top with the sparkling wine. Garnish with a strip of cucumber rolled in a circle and secured with a cocktail pick.

MAKES 1 COCKTAIL

Kiwi Kiss

Lemon, ginger, and the tart freshness of the kiwi fruit come together in this delectably crisp cocktail. Be sure to use kiwis that are ripe (but not so soft that they have wrinkles) to give your cocktail the most flavor.

1 kiwi fruit, peeled and sliced

¾ ounce Lemongrass-Ginger Syrup (page 96)

½ ounce soju (see page 39)

6 ounces dry sparkling sake, such as Zipang (see Resources, page 111)

1 thick slice of kiwi, cut into a square, for garnish

6-inch section of fresh lemongrass, cleaned and peeled, for garnish

Add the peeled kiwi slices to a rocks glass along with the Lemongrass-Ginger Syrup and soju. Using a muddler, mash the kiwi. Fill the glass three-quarters full with ice. Top with the sparkling sake. Use a metal cocktail pick to make a hole through the square slice of kiwi. Thread the kiwi slice onto the lemongrass "spear" as a garnish.

MAKES 1 COCKTAIL

Blueberry Caipirinha

The caipirinha (ky-per-EEN-yuh), which means "little peasant girl" in Portuguese, is the national cocktail of Brazil. It's traditionally made with limes, sugar, and a sugarcane liquor called *cachaça* (kuh-SHAH-suh), but it's great with other fruit flavors. Cachaça—the third most popular spirit in the world—can have an unrefined flavor, so look for brands such as Mae de Ouro or Sagatiba, which have a clean, slightly herbal taste.

12 fresh blueberries

6 slices of lime

2 teaspoons brown sugar

1 ounce cachaça

3 or 4 ounces chilled brut cava

1 thin slice of lime, for garnish

1 blueberry, for garnish

Put the blueberries and lime slices in a rocks glass. Muddle until the berries are mashed and the lime has released its juice. Add the brown sugar and cachaça and stir to dissolve the sugar. Fill the glass two-thirds full with ice. Add the cava. To garnish, wrap the thin slice of lime around the blueberry and anchor with a cocktail pick.

MAKES 1 COCKTAIL

HAPPY ENDINGS

I DON'T FEEL AS IF A MEAL HAS ENDED
PROPERLY UNLESS I HAVE A TASTE OF
SOMETHING SWEET.

There's no better way to end a meal than with a
glass of zingy and slightly sweet sparkling wine or
champagne. Taking this one step farther, all the
recipes in this chapter capture the bright and crisp
quality of sparkling wines and use them in a variety
of satisfying and light desserts. Any of these recipes
can be made by popping open a fresh bottle of
bubbly, but to me it makes more sense to create
them with that extra cup or so of champagne left
over from the night before.

Lemon Ice

This is a dessert cocktail most commonly found around Venice, where it's called S'groppino. The lemon, mint, and vodka act as a digestif, making this cocktail a light and refreshing way to end a meal. It's also delicious with gin instead of vodka.

    4   ounces prosecco
    ¾   ounce vodka
    1   tablespoon softened lemon sorbet
    1   fresh mint leaf, torn in pieces

Add the prosecco and vodka to a champagne flute. Add the sorbet. Sprinkle with the torn mint and serve immediately.

MAKES 1 COCKTAIL

CHAMPAGNE HEADACHES

One bottle of champagne contains more than 250 million bubbles. And it's not your imagination that bubbly goes to your head faster than a glass of chardonnay does. A study at the University of Surrey in Guildford, Surrey, England, found that the CO_2 speeds up the absorption of alcohol in the body. So not only do you feel tipsy faster when drinking champagne; the effects last longer than do the effects of still wine.

Sipping champagne through a straw—a practice that models started at fashion shows to save their lipstick—also makes the champagne more potent because of the extra air ingested. The bottom line? Moderation is key!

Sparkling Pineapple Push-Ups

The bright flavor of pineapple mixed with lemongrass and ginger gives these frozen treats a slightly exotic flair. If you want to make a nonalcoholic version, just substitute your favorite sparkling water for the wine.

    1   cup fresh pineapple juice
    1   tablespoon Lemongrass-Ginger Syrup (page 96)
    ½   cup brut sparkling wine
        Push-up Popsicle mold (see Resources, page 111)

In a measuring cup, combine the pineapple juice, syrup, and sparkling wine. Mix with a spoon to dissolve the syrup thoroughly.

Pour the pineapple mixture into the 6 cavities of a push-up Popsicle mold. Insert the caps and sticks in the Popsicle mold. Be sure to leave at least ¾ inch at the top, as the push-ups will expand as they freeze.

Freeze for 4 hours or until solid.

MAKES 6 POPSICLES

Champagne Snow Cones

This adult version of a snow cone can be made using the granita method (described below), in a sorbet machine, or in a shaved-ice machine (see Resources, page 111), which gives the ice a fluffy texture. Serve in vintage champagne coupes, if you have them. Set the dessert table with a variety of Torani flavored syrups (see Resources, page 111), fruit liqueurs, and herb-infused syrups in pretty bottles and let your guests flavor their snow cones as they like.

⅛ cup sugar

Juice of ½ lemon, strained

1 teaspoon lemon zest

1¾ cups champagne or sparkling wine

Assorted flavored syrups and liqueurs

In a medium-size nonreactive pot, heat 1¾ cups water and the sugar, stirring until the sugar dissolves. Add the lemon juice and zest and the champagne.

Let the mixture cool to room temperature. If you have a snow-cone maker, use it to freeze the champagne mixture according to the manufacturer's instructions.

If not using a snow-cone maker, follow the granita method. Pour the liquid into a shallow metal or glass pan and place it in the freezer for 2 hours. Once the liquid starts to harden, remove from the freezer and fluff the ice crystals with a fork. Smooth them back down and return the pan to the freezer, this time letting it set for another hour or so. Fluff the champagne ice once again with a fork and then smooth it back down and return the pan to the freezer. Let the ice freeze solid. Just before serving, fluff up again with a fork.

Use an ice-cream scoop to add the champagne ice to a footed dessert glass or champagne coupe. Let guests drizzle their snow cones with the flavored syrups and liqueurs of their choice. Accompany with long-handled iced-tea spoons.

MAKES 5 CUPS

CHAMPAGNE COUPE

There's a well-known rumor that the perky breasts of a famous French beauty inspired the short champagne glass called the coupe. In another tale, the seductress Madame de Pompadour is said to have had coupes molded from her breasts because her lover, King Louis XV, longed to drink champagne from them. Unfortunately, the stories associated with the champagne coupe may be their best attribute. The shallow sides of the coupe allow the bubbles in champagne to dissipate very quickly, so the coupe is not considered the best choice for serving sparkling wines. These days, one of the best ways to use your grandmother's champagne coupes is for serving dessert or retro cocktails.

Raspberry Lychee Parfait

Raspberries, lychee, and rosewater make a seductive combination in this parfait inspired by a dessert at Alain Ducasse's Mix in Las Vegas. Serve this with a long-handled iced-tea spoon. The idea is to experience different flavors and textures in one spoonful.

½ cup sparkling wine

½ cup lychee juice

1 packet unflavored gelatin

½ cup fresh raspberries (reserve 2 for the garnish)

2 teaspoons framboise (raspberry dessert wine)

2 tablespoons Monin lychee syrup (see Resources, page 111)

1 cup whipping cream

2 tablespoons rosewater

2 tablespoons sugar

In a small sauce pot, bring the sparkling wine and ¼ cup of the lychee juice to a boil. Pour the remaining ¼ cup of lychee juice in a tempered glass mixing cup. Sprinkle with the gelatin and let sit for a few minutes so the gelatin softens.

Place ¼ cup of the raspberries in the bottom of each of 2 parfait glasses. Drizzle each with 1 teaspoon of framboise.

Once the wine and lychee juice come to a boil, remove from the heat and stir into the softened gelatin mixture. Stir to dissolve the gelatin completely, about 5 minutes. Add the lychee syrup.

Pour ½ cup of the gelatin mixture into each of the prepared parfait glasses. The raspberries will rise to the top. Set the glasses inside a square baking pan. Place the pan in the refrigerator until the gelatin sets, about 2 hours or overnight, if you like. Make sure the pan is level or your parfaits will be crooked.

Just before serving, pour the whipping cream into a chilled bowl and beat the cream. Keep beating and as the cream starts to get fluffy add the rosewater and the sugar.

Garnish each parfait with a healthy dollop of whipped cream and a raspberry.

MAKES 2 PARFAITS

Pomegranate Passion Float

This colorful spirited float would be the perfect addition to a bridal shower or brunch menu. Once you master this recipe, use it as a guide to create your own floats with a combination of sparkling wine, liqueur, and sorbet. Be sure to use an intensely flavored sorbet that has a high fruit content and is not super-sweet.

1	ounce Pama pomegranate liqueur
3 to 4	ounces sparkling wine
1	scoop of passion fruit sorbet

Pour the pomegranate liqueur into a champagne flute. Add the sparkling wine. There should be at least 1 inch at the top of the glass to make room for the sorbet. Use a round measuring tablespoon to make a nice ball of sorbet, then add it to the glass.

MAKES 1 COCKTAIL

VARIATIONS

Try different flavor combinations; the possibilities are endless. Here are some ideas:

- Alizé and passion fruit sorbet
- Limoncello and raspberry sorbet
- Domaine de Canton ginger liqueur and peach sorbet

Grapefruit Vanilla Granita

I like making this granita with rosé sparkling wine, because the color enhances the pale pink of the grapefruit; but you can use any sparkling wine you have on hand.

¾	cup grapefruit juice, strained
¾	cup brut rosé sparkling wine
½	vanilla bean, split lengthwise
⅛	cup Torani pink grapefruit syrup (see Resources, page 111)
⅛	cup vanilla-infused vodka or soju

Heat the grapefruit juice, sparkling wine, and vanilla bean in a small nonreactive pot over medium heat. After about 4 minutes, remove the mixture from the heat and add the grapefruit syrup and vanilla vodka or soju.

Let cool to room temperature. Pour the liquid into a shallow pan and cover. Let freeze for two hours. Once it hardens, remove from the freezer and use a fork to fluff the granita. Return to the freezer for another hour or so and fluff once more. Let the granita rest in the freezer for another hour. To serve, fluff the granita again and serve in small bowls.

MAKES 2 CUPS

Peach Elderflower Gelée

The fragrance of elderflower and flavor of ripe peach in this simple gelatin pair wonderfully with Moscato d'Asti, although any sparkling wine or champagne will do. Pour into delicate four-ounce footed glasses to make a lovely dessert after a luncheon. This recipe would also work well with ripe apricots or nectarines or with pitted white cherries.

1 cup Moscato d'Asti or other sweet sparkling wine

1 ripe peach, washed and cubed

1 packet unflavored gelatin

2 tablespoons white elderflower syrup (see Resources, page 111) or St-Germain elderflower liqueur

1 tablespoon sugar

Bring ¾ cup of the sparkling wine to a boil in a small sauce pot. Reserve ¼ cup in the refrigerator.

Meanwhile, divide the cubed peach evenly among the 4 dessert glasses.

Pour the ¼ cup of chilled sparkling wine into a tempered glass mixing cup. Sprinkle with the gelatin and let sit for a minute. Add the hot wine and then stir to dissolve the gelatin; let sit for 5 minutes. Add the elderflower syrup or liqueur and sugar, stirring to dissolve completely.

Pour ¼ cup of the gelatin mixture over the peaches in each of the 4 dessert glasses. Set the glasses inside a square baking pan and place in the refrigerator until the gelatin sets, about 2 hours or overnight, if you like. Make sure the pan is level, or your gelée will be crooked.

Remove the desserts from the refrigerator 30 minutes before serving, so the gelée is a little less firm.

MAKES 4 SERVINGS

MIXER RECIPES

MAKING YOUR OWN SOUR MIX, FLAVORED

SYRUPS, AND INFUSED SPIRITS

IS SURPRISINGLY EASY.

And once you compare these versions to the ones

sold in stores, you'll be convinced. They'll give your

cocktails a distinctive flavor, and you'll find that

they have other uses, too. The rose geranium and

lemongrass-ginger syrups can be added to sparkling

water to make Italian sodas; the black pepper syrup

is good served over melon, berries, and vanilla

ice cream. The small amount of time and the fresh

ingredients you put into these mixers will pay off

when you see how pleased your guests are.

Homemade Sour Mix

Sure you can buy sour mix at the store, but if you take a little time to make your own, you'll see that it has a bright and fresh taste that you can't find in a bottle. It's also more economical and you know that it doesn't contain any artificial flavorings or ingredients.

1 cup sugar
1 cup combination of fresh lime juice and
   lemon juice

Add 1 cup water and the sugar to a non-reactive 2-quart pot and bring to a boil. Let cool slightly, then add the lemon-lime juice and stir. Let cool, then pour through a funnel into a sterilized bottle. Store in the refrigerator for up to one week.

MAKES 1½ CUPS

Lemongrass-Ginger Syrup

Using fresh lemongrass with purplish rings and young gingerroot that's pale gold in color will ensure this syrup has lots of flavor. It's also great used in hot tea or added to lemonade.

1 cup sugar
½ cup peeled and sliced fresh gingerroot
½ cup peeled and sliced fresh lemongrass

Add 1 cup water and the sugar to a 2-quart pot and bring to a boil. Lower the heat, add the gingerroot and lemongrass, and simmer for 25 minutes. The syrup will be slightly golden and fragrant when done.

Remove from the heat and let cool. Remove the pieces of lemongrass and ginger from the syrup. Using a funnel, pour the cooled syrup into a sterilized glass bottle. Store in the refrigerator for up to one month.

MAKES 1¼ CUPS

Black Pepper Syrup

In addition to adding a spicy note to the Fraise des Bois cocktail on page 77, this syrup is delicious served on melon, berries, or vanilla ice cream.

  1 cup sugar

1½ tablespoons freshly ground black pepper

Add 1 cup water and the sugar to a 2-quart pot and bring to a boil. Lower the heat, add the black pepper, and simmer for 15 minutes. The syrup will be golden and fragrant when done.

Remove from the heat and let cool. Set a strainer over a funnel and pour the cooled syrup into a sterilized glass bottle. Store in the refrigerator for up to one month.

MAKES 1¼ CUPS

Thyme Syrup

Use this aromatic syrup in the Tangerine Dream cocktail on page 39, or to add an herbal note to any cocktail using citrus.

  ¾ cup sugar

20 sprigs of fresh thyme, washed

Add ¾ cup water and the sugar to a 2-quart pot and bring to a boil. Lower the heat, add the thyme, and simmer for 15 minutes. The syrup will be slightly golden and fragrant when done.

Remove from the heat and let cool. Set a strainer over a funnel and pour the cooled syrup into a sterilized glass bottle. Store in the refrigerator for up to one month.

MAKES 1 GENEROUS CUP

Rose Geranium Syrup

This syrup has a citrusy rose aroma and flavor that is good in the Bubbling Blackberry Bramble on page 78 and with red fruits of all sorts. Be sure to use leaves that have not been sprayed with pesticides.

¾ cup sugar

20 rose geranium leaves, washed and patted dry

Add ¾ cup water and the sugar to a 2-quart pot and bring to a boil. Lower the heat, add the rose geranium leaves, and simmer for 15 minutes. The syrup will be slightly golden and fragrant when done.

Remove from the heat and let cool. Using a funnel, pour the cooled syrup into a sterilized glass bottle. Store in the refrigerator for up to one month.

MAKES 1 GENEROUS CUP

Vanilla-Infused Soju

I made my own vanilla-infused liquor because I couldn't find a commercial product that had a real vanilla flavor. It couldn't have been easier.

Set the bottle in a sunny spot while the vanilla bean steeps. You can keep pouring on more soju or vodka as you use it for a while. Use a new bean when the liquor's vanilla fragrance starts to wane. Soju is a distilled Asian spirit made from rice or sweet potatoes.

1 cup soju (see page 39)

1 vanilla bean, split lengthwise

Put the vanilla bean in a sterilized jar with a stopper. Pour in the cup of soju, or enough to cover the vanilla bean. Let it steep for 2 or 3 days, until it takes on a strong vanilla aroma. Pour into a bottle. Keeps indefinitely.

MAKES 1 CUP

APPENDIX

BUBBLY GUIDE TO CHAMPAGNE AND SPARKLING WINE

What to Know Before You Sip

A glass of bubbly tastes perfectly delicious—even if you have no idea how it was made. But I'm sure at least once you've been a little curious about this magical drink that is the only wine in the world that can be enjoyed with all five senses. Here's a quick primer on how those bubbles wind up in the bottle.

Grapes are harvested and crushed to release their juice. The sugar and yeast in the grape juice ferment and become alcohol, turning that grape juice into wine. But before this wine can become sparkling wine or champagne, it must go through another transformation to add carbon dioxide (CO_2) bubbles into it. This usually happens one of three ways, no matter where sparkling wines are produced in the world.

The most famous way for wine to become bubbly is through a secondary fermentation in the bottle, often called *méthode champenoise* (may-TOHD sham-pen-WAAZ). The term literally means "the Champagne method." Wine from a combination of chardonnay, pinot noir, and pinot meunier grapes is blended with other batches of wine from up to one hundred different vineyards to create the flavor profile the winemaker wants. Then the wine is put into bottles, along with a little yeast and sugar. This starts a second fermentation that gives off CO_2 gas. This gas, trapped inside the bottle, is what gives the wine its tiny bubbles. The phrases *méthode traditionelle* and "fermented in this bottle" mean the same thing as *méthode champenoise*.

In *charmat* (shar-MOTT), a method that's faster and less costly than *méthode champenoise,* wine is put into a large glass-lined tank. A mixture of yeast and sugar is added and the temperature is increased until the wine becomes bubbly. The wine is then bottled as a sparkling wine. This method is used to make wines with delicate fruit and floral aromas such as prosecco and Moscato d'Asti.

Carbonation is the least expensive and least desirable way to make a sparkling wine. The wine is pumped full of carbon dioxide, just the same as with soda pop. The bubbles in this wine will be large.

A fourth method, known by the French term *méthode ancestrale* (may-TOHD ann-ses-TRAAL), is an old method that is not used often except in small areas in France by Vin du Bugey Cerdon and Clairette de Die and in California by Toad Hollow for HS Risqué sparkling wine. Grapes are picked by hand, pressed, and fermented in vats until the resulting wine has about 6 percent alcohol. The wine is bottled, and it finishes fermenting inside the bottle, which makes the wine bubbly.

Understanding Wine Styles

Knowing what wine terms mean can help you choose a wine that will please your palate. The following list is organized from sweet to not-so-sweet wines. Because it's difficult to imagine what some of these styles of wine taste like, I've compared them to lemonade, which is all about a balance between tart and sweet and helps provide a familiar frame of reference.

Doux: Pronounced "doo," it means straight-up sweet, like lemonade made by someone who got carried away with the sugar scoop. Though the best are balanced by vibrant natural acidity, these wines could double for dessert as they have at least 5 percent sugar.

Super sips: Inniskillin Sparkling Vidal Ice Wine, Banfi Rosa Regale Brachetto d'Acqui, Mionetto Sparkling Moscato d'Asti

Demi-sec: Pronounced "demi sek." The phrase means "half-dry" and refers to wines with 3.3 to 5 percent sugar. That's another way of saying half as sweet as doux, but still pretty sweet, like a sugary glass of lemonade.

Super sips: Moët et Chandon Nectar Imperial, Schramsberg Crémant, Gruet Demi-sec

Dry or Sec: Like a perfect glass of lemonade, these wines have a noticeable amount of sugar ranging from 1.7 to 3.5 percent, though there's tanginess on the finish. They're not so popular anymore; most wines are either sweeter or more dry.

Super sips: Taittinger Nocturne Sec N.V., Mumm Napa Cuvée M

Extra Dry: These wines have a hint of sweetness, with 1.2 to 2 percent sugar. Using the lemonade comparison, the lemon is more noticeable. They are crowd pleasers; secretly, most Americans prefer extra-dry wines, though they say they like their champagne brut. That's probably why Moët's Imperial is the top-selling champagne in the United States.

Super sips: Moët et Chandon Imperial, Domaine Chandon Riche, Domaine Sainte-Michelle Extra Dry Sparkling Wine

Brut: Pronounced "broot," this classic style of wine is straightforward and blunt with its crisp acidity and a hint of toastiness. With less than 1.5 percent sugar, it's like a cleansing glass of lemon water. This is the most popular style of wine for most wineries; the starting-level wine is their non-vintage brut.

Super sips: Iron Horse Sonoma Classic Vintage Brut, Roederer Estate NV Brut, Laurent-Perrier Champagne Brut

Extra Brut: This style of wine is even more in-your-face than brut. This style is also called Brut Nature or Brut Sauvage. At less than 0.6 percent sugar, it's so crisp and acidic that a sip might remind you of a straight shot of lemon juice. Not so bad if you're eating smoked salmon, but this wine might be a bit harsh on its own.

Super sips: Tarlant Brut Zero, Korbel Brut Nature, Jacquesson Extra Brut

American Sparkling Wines

Large and small producers craft sparkling wines in nearly every state of the United States where wine is made. Wineries offer every style of wine, from sparkling moscatos to blanc de blancs to good dry rosés. Here are some of the notable areas and winemakers whose production is readily available.

CENTRAL CALIFORNIA

Laetitia: If you're passing through Arroyo Grande in San Luis Obispo County, definitely stop and taste some of the elegant but boldly flavored sparkling wines made in the French style at Laetitia.

Super sip: Laetitia NV Brut Rosé

NORTHERN CALIFORNIA

Domaine Carneros: Set in a French-style chateau on a hill, this winery owned by Taittinger produces sparkling wines that burst with expressive California fruit flavors and bright acidity balanced by a toasty quality that seems more French. CEO and winemaker Eileen Crane has made sparkling wines longer than anyone in the United States.

Super sips: Le Rêve Blanc de Blancs, Brut Rosé

Domaine Chandon: This winery owned by Moët et Chandon produces a range of well-crafted wines that are affordable and tend to offer bolder flavors that are made to pair with food. Their Étoile line offers a more refined taste

profile. Other attractions include the gorgeously landscaped grounds and a fine-dining restaurant serving seasonal cuisine paired with sparkling wines and bubbly cocktails.

Super sips: Domaine Chandon Riche, Chandon Rosé, Étoile Brut

Gloria Ferrer: This is the California winery of the Spanish wine company Freixenet, the largest sparkling wine producer in the world. It's named after the wife of founder José Ferrer. They produce a range of wines with subtle character.

Super sip: Royal Cuvée

Iron Horse: Rustic and beautiful grounds surround this family-owned winery in the heart of Sonoma's Green Valley. Founders Barry and Audrey Sterling are considered pioneers in California sparkling wine and their daughter Joy is known for the fun events she arranges for winery club members. Iron Horse creates lean and elegant wines that are carefully handled in the winery so they taste precisely like the area where the grapes were grown.

Super sips: Brut Rosé, Wedding Cuvée, Joy

J Wine: Judy Jordan's sleek and modern winery in Sonoma County produces complexly flavored sparkling wines. The winery specializes in showing how their wines pair with food by offering tastings of gourmet food served in their garden café or Bubble Room salon.

Super sip: J Cuvée 20 Brut

Korbel: Surrounded by massive redwoods and colorful landscaping, the winery at the north end of Sonoma County was established in 1882 by the

Korbel brothers from Czechoslovakia. Their family name is Czech for "goblet" or "cup." All of their wines, which range from a popular extra-dry wine to sparkling merlot only available at the winery, are produced by the *méthode champenoise.*

Super sips: Extra Dry, Brut Rosé

Mumm Napa: An extensive tour that shows off the winemaking process is a highlight at this large winery owned by the French champagne house G. H. Mumm. The wines balance California fruit character with French techniques.

Super sips: DVX, Cuvée M

Roederer Estate: Set off a winding road in Anderson Valley, this is the California winery of the French champagne house Louis Roederer. All of their wines have a crisp note of green apple attributed to the cool climate. Try their brut in a 750 milliliter bottle and magnum; you won't believe the difference the bigger bottle makes.

Super sip: Brut in magnum

Schramsberg: Jack and Jamie Davies became pioneers in the field of American sparkling wine when they moved to a historic Victorian home and winery in northern Napa County in the late 1960s and began making bubbly in the fine French tradition. Their son Hugh now runs the winery, which is known for approachable and food-friendly wines.

Super sips: J Schram, Blanc de Noirs

SOUTHERN CALIFORNIA

Thornton Winery: Located in the scenic Temecula Valley—a popular Southern California wine tourism destination—the winery is owned by San Diego power couple John and Sally Thornton. It produces a range of sparkling wines according to the *méthode champenoise.*

Super sip: Thornton Cuvée Rouge

MICHIGAN

L. Mawby: Tucked away in the chilly Leelanau Peninsula of northern Michigan, Larry Mawby's winery uses native grapes like vignoles and seyval to make two lines of sparkling wines: a serious *méthode champenoise* wine under the L. Mawby label and a more affordable *charmat* method wine under M. Lawrence. The wines are readily available in Michigan, and they can be mail-ordered from the winery if allowed by your state.

Super sips: Fizz, Sex

NEW MEXICO

Gruet: Gilbert Gruet, who had run a winery in Champagne since 1952, was vacationing in New Mexico when he learned that the region near Albuquerque was ideal for growing grapes. He planted mountain vineyards with pinot noir and chardonnay as an experiment. The family has since won many awards for their refined, French-style wines.

Super sips: Brut Rosé, Blanc de Noirs

OREGON

Argyle: Tucked away in the hills outside of Portland, Argyle produces brut sparkling wines from locally grown chardonnay and pinot noir.

Super sip: Knudsen Vineyard Brut

Soter: Tony Soter's love of the pinot noir grape is evident in his elegant, French-style sparkling wines crafted from Yamhill County fruit.

Super sips: Beacon Hill Brut Rosé, Blanc de Blancs

WASHINGTON

Domaine Ste. Michelle: Ever since their first sparkling wine was released in 1978, this winery in the Columbia Valley has had a reputation for producing well-crafted wines at remarkably affordable prices.

Super sips: Luxe Blanc de Blancs, DSM Extra Dry Sparkling Wine

French Champagnes and Sparkling Wines

CHAMPAGNE

The first sparkling wines of Champagne were thought to be an accident. Monks who were trying to make still white wines thought their wines were cursed because they started to bubble.

Because the Champagne region is located in the north, it often got so cold while grapes were fermenting that the yeast stopped working. The monks then bottled the wine and put it away to age. In the spring, when the wine warmed up, the yeast started working again, creating carbon dioxide bubbles in the wine.

Regardless of whether the monk Dom Pérignon ever said "Come quickly brothers, I am drinking stars," he didn't invent champagne. But he definitely did a lot to refine the process of making champagne and to transform it from a mistake into a desirable indulgence enjoyed by royalty.

Three grape varieties may be used to make champagne: pinot noir, chardonnay, and a dark-skinned grape called pinot meunier. Hundreds of champagnes are made in the Champagne region, but only a very small number ever reach the market in the United States. Champagne, because of its association with luxury and status, is one of the most heavily marketed and branded products in the world.

The luxury-goods conglomerate Louis Vuitton Moët Hennessy produces some of the best-known high-end champagnes: Veuve Clicquot, Moët et Chandon, Krug, Ruinart, and Dom Pérignon. Other grand champagne houses worth knowing include Bollinger, Laurent-Perrier, Louis Roederer, Nicolas Feuillatte, Pol Roger, Pommery, and Taittinger.

Many champagne connoisseurs prefer to seek out wines made by smaller wineries that produce a fine product but spend more on winemaking than on marketing, such as Alfred Gratien, Audoin de Dampierre, Billecart-Salmon, Demoiselle, Fleury, Gosset, Henriot, Jacquesson, Gaston Chiquet, Ployez-Jacquemart, and Trouillard.

SPARKLING WINES

Clairette de Die (clay-RETT duh dee): This white, gently sparkling wine from the Rhône often is made with a combination of muscat blanc and clairette grapes. It can have a hint of sweetness.

Super sips: Cave Carod, Domaine Achard-Vincent

Crémant d'Alsace (kray-MONT doll-SOSS): A general term for sparkling wines from Alsace, these are considered some of the finest sparkling wines in all of France. Made from pinot noir, pinot blanc, and pinot auxerrois grapes, the best are a clear expression of the region's cool climate and mineral soil and are surprisingly affordable.

Super sips: Joseph Pfister, Lucien Albrecht, Charles Baur

Crémant de Bourgogne (kray-MONT duh bore-GONYE): A general term for sparkling wines from Burgundy, these wines can be made from a number of grapes including chardonnay and pinot noir—two of the grapes used in champagne—as well as pinot gris and gamay. The best are well crafted and are amazing value wines.

Super sips: Blason de Bourgogne, Louis Bouillot, Veuve Ambal, Simonnet-Febvre

Crémant de Limoux (kray-MONT duh lee-MOO)/**Blanquette** (blawn-KETT) **de Limoux:** It's believed that France's first sparkling wine originated in the Limoux region of the Languedoc-Rousillon back in the 1530s. Crémant de Limoux is mostly a blend of chardonnay and chenin blanc that is well aged. Blanquette de Limoux is mostly made from the local mauzac grape and is not aged as long.

Super sips: Aimery Sieur d'Arques, J. Laurens, Saint-Hilaire, Domaine de Martinolles

Crémant de Loire (kray-MONT duh lwar): This term refers to the many sparkling wines made in the Saumur, Touraine, and Anjou regions of the Loire Valley. These dry wines are mostly based on chenin blanc and sometimes balanced with chardonnay or cabernet franc. With racy acidity, they are less bubbly than champagne, giving a smoothness on the palate.

Super sips: Langlois-Château, Bouvet-Ladubay, Domaine des Baumard, Tessier

Sparkling Vouvray: Made from chenin blanc in the Loire Valley, these softly sparkling wines are crisp with fruity notes of melon, peach, and honey balanced by good acidity and mineral notes. Ranging from brut to slightly sweet, sparkling Vouvrays are very food-friendly, especially with spicy food or richer seafood like lobster.

Super sips: Champalou, Château Moncontour, Domaine des Aubuisières

Txakoli (CHA-ko-ly): A lightly sparkling, fresh wine from the Basque country in southwestern France and northern Spain. White txakoli is made from Hondarribi Zuri and Folle Blanche grapes. It is a rare treat; try it with seafood. Also called txakolina (cha-ko-LEE-na).

Super sips: Gorka Izagirre, Txomin Etxaniz, Ameztod

Vin du Bugey-Cerdon (van doo boo-JHEE sair-DON): This is a general term for the delightful and uncomplicated rosé wines produced in the tiny region between Lyons and Geneva. Often made from gamay, the wines are slightly sweet with a good balance of tartness and flavors of cranberries, raspberries, and strawberries.

Super sips: Bottex, Lingot-Martin, Domaine Renardat-Fâche, Caveau du Mont July

Italian Sparkling Wines

No wonder Italians know how to live the dolce vita. More sparkling wines are made in Italy than in any other country in the world. Most of these wines are lower in alcohol, which gives them a light quality, and many are also quite affordable. The best Italian sparklers will say either DOC or DOCG on the label, which means they conform to a set of quality standards for their home region.

Brachetto d'Acqui (brah-keh-toe DA-kwee): Made from a dark-skinned grape from the Piedmont region of Italy. It is usually made into a sweet, lightly sparkling wine balanced with good acidity and aromas and flavors of cranberries, raspberries, and roses.

Super sips: Banfi, Ca' dei Mandorli, Pineto

Erbaluce di Caluso (er-ba-LOO-chy dee cah-LOO-so): An ancient grape from Piedmont, its name means "dawn light," because of the peachy hue of the ripe grapes. The high-acid grape produces pale green wines that taste of peaches, pears, and lemon.

Super sips: Orsolani, Cieck

Fragolino (frah-go-LEE-no): This is an uncomplicated wine made from the fragola grape in various regions of northern Italy including Friuli, Trentino, and Tuscany. It's mostly sweet and tastes like strawberries.

Super sips: Torciano, Nando

Franciacorta (fran-CHA-kore-tuh): This is a crisp, brut-style white wine that comes from the premier winemaking region in Lombardy. Made from a blend of chardonnay, pinot blanc, and pinot noir, these wines are a pale gold-green color and show a remarkable freshness, though they are made with the *méthode champenoise.*

Super sips: Ca' del Bosco, Bellavista, Cavalleri

Gavi (GAH-vee): The cortese grape grown near the town of Gavi makes gently sparkling wines that are fruity with aromas of peaches, lime, and melon.

Super sips: Vigne Regali, La Scolca

Lambrusco (lam-BROOS-koh): A red or white sparkling wine from Italy's Emilia-Romagna region, it has a dual identity. Many of the Lambruscos on the market in the United States are inexpensive and sweet, but Italians treasure the well-made dry Lambruscos.

Super sips: Ca' de' Medici, Medici Ermete, Lini, Vittorio Graziano, Ca' Berti

Malvasia (mal-va-SEE-yuh): This is a white or rosé wine from the Emilia-Romagna region. It is usually dry and has a rich aroma that smells like peaches, melon, and nutmeg.

Super sips: Ariola, La Stoppa

Moscato d'Asti (moe-SKA-toh DOS-tee): This is the top-quality, lightly sparkling wine made from the moscato grape in Piedmont. The best wines from the region will be labeled Moscato d'Asti. It's closely related to an Asti or Asti Spumante, a less expensive wine that's sweeter and more bubbly than Moscato d'Asti.

Super sips: Ceretto Mionetto, Saracco, Michele Chiarlo

Prosecco (pro-SEKKO): A light sparkling wine from the Veneto of northern Italy. It has a fresh aroma like citrus and honeysuckle and a taste that's a little mineral. The best proseccos will mention the towns of Conegliano or Valdobbiadene on the label, or Cartizze, the grand hilltop vineyard.

Super sips: Bisol, Mionetto, Villa Sandi, Drusian

The Rest of the World
AUSTRALIA

Australian wine makers produce a variety of sparkling wines, including Tasmanian stand-outs Jansz and Frogmore Creek, but the best-known export is deep-purple sparkling shiraz. Made in Australia since the 1860s, its production was started by an expatriate Frenchman. A good one tastes of chocolate, cherries, and warm spices and has a little bite of tannin. In Australia, it's the traditional wine to pair with turkey on Christmas.

Super sips: Rumball, Fox Creek, Wyndham Estate

GERMANY

Sparkling wines are made from a variety of grapes including the national favorite Riesling, chardonnay, and pinot noir; all of them are called *sekt,* which means "sparkling." The best sekt (pronounced "zekt") often stays in Germany, but a few wines are available internationally.

Super sips: Raumland, Fitz-Ritter, Studert-Prüm

GREECE

The ancient moschofilero (mos-koh-FEE-lero) grape produces refreshing wines that are great with Mediterranean-style food. A good one has hints of citrus and smells a little like rose.

Super sips: Domaine Spiropolous, Tselepos, Boutari

JAPAN

Sparkling sake is made from rice just like other sakes, but the fermentation is stopped early, when there is still some sugar in the rice mash. The liquid finishes fermentation in the bottle, causing the sake to become bubbly. Sparkling sake typically has 5 to 10 percent alcohol.

Super sips: Zipang, Suzune, Hou Hou Shu

PORTUGAL

The native spritzy wine of Portugal is called *vinho verde* ("green wine") because it is made from slightly under-ripe grapes, such as alvarinho. Look for one with a recent vintage year, as these are meant to be drunk young.

Super sips: Cruzeiro Lima, Mesa do Presidente, Adega Dante deLinea

SPAIN

Spanish for "cave," *cava* is a sparkling wine from the Penedes region that is made the same way as champagne but using three native grapes: xarel-lo, macabeo, and parellada. It has become popular for its lightness tinged with citrus, flowers, and mineral notes.

Super sips: Segura Viudas, Marques de Gelida, Cava Can Vendrell, 1+1=3, Albet i Noya

Organic Sparkling Wines and Champagnes

With the growing market for organic products, it's no surprise that more people want wine made without chemical fertilizers and pesticides. Vintners worldwide are meeting that demand with all-natural sparkling wines and champagnes. Domaine Carneros in Napa recently became the first major sparkling-wine producer to have its vineyards certified organic. There are shades of difference between the terms organic wine, wine made from organic grapes, and biodynamic wine, but all come from vineyards that are certified to be free from chemicals. The Organic Wine Company (theorganicwinecompany.com), diamondorganics.com, and ecoexpress.com offer organic bubbly.

Here are some others that are available:

UNITED STATES
- Jeriko Estate (Brut and Brut Rosé)
- La Rocca Vineyards (Brut Blanc de Blancs)

FRANCE
- Delmas (Blanquette de Limoux Brut and Crémant de Limoux Brut)
- Fleury Champagne (Carte Rouge Brut and Brut Rosé)
- Serge Faust Champagne (Carte d'Or Brut)

ITALY
- Mario Torelli (Moscato d'Asti and Brut)
- Perlage (Riva Moretta prosecco)

SPAIN
- Albet i Noya (Cava Brut 21 and Cava Can Vendrell Brut Reserva)
- Privat (Cava Laietà Reserva Brut Nature)

Exceptional Wines

The price of a bottle of sparkling wine or champagne is determined by several factors: the price of the grapes that went into the wine, the rarity of the wine, and the producer's reputation. Here are some wines worth the splurge.

Billecart-Salmon: There's a perfect balance to this dry rosé made by a small, distinguished house. It's a deep salmon color with rich flavors of raspberries, plums, and toast. About $85.

Krug Grande Cuvée: From the grapes selected to the way it's fermented in wood and aged, this wine is unique in every sense. About $130.

Bollinger Blanc de Noirs Vielles Vignes: Very few producers in Champagne make a blanc de noirs, a wine made exclusively from pinot noir grapes. This wine is made only in extra-ordinary years and from old vines, which produce fewer grapes with amazing flavor. About $600.

Henriot Cuvée des Enchanteleurs: Named for the workers who watch over special casks of wine, this wine is delicate with aromas and flavors of dried fruits, mushrooms, and earth. About $140.

Inniskillin Sparkling Vidal Eiswein: It takes hundreds of pounds of frozen grapes to produce this Canadian wine that tastes like honey, ripe apricots, and peaches. About $90 for 375 ml.

Krug Clos de Mesnil: Produced from chardon-nay grapes grown in what is considered one of the best vineyards in all of Champagne. About $700.

Salon Blanc de Blancs: Considered the most precious champagne in the world because it is made in very small quantities and all the grapes come from the famous vineyards Clos de Mesnil. About $250.

Recommended Wines by Price

You can expect to pay anywhere from $10 to $55 for a basic bottle of bubbly—called *nonvintage brut* by most wineries. The starting-level brut wine is a good place to find out if you like the style before investing in a more costly wine.

SECRET SIPS: $10 OR LESS

- Korbel Brut
- Rotari Brut Arte Italiana
- Domaine Ste. Michelle Brut

FROM $10 TO $15

- Bouvet-Ladubay NV Brut
- Louis Bouillot
- Mionetto Prosecco Brut NV
- Piper Sonoma Cellars NV Brut
- Segura Viudas Aria Estate Brut
- Zardetto NV Prosecco Brut

FROM $15 TO $20

- Argyle Brut
- Domaine Chandon NV Brut Classic

- Gruet NV Brut
- Gloria Ferrer NV Brut
- Lucien Albrecht Cremant d'Alsace Brut NV
- Marques de Gelida Cava
- Mumm Napa Brut Prestige
- Schramsberg Mirabelle NV Brut

FROM $20 TO 30

- Domaine Carneros Brut
- Iron Horse Classic Vintage Brut
- J Cuvée 20 Brut
- Laetitia Brut Cuvée
- Roederer Estate NV Brut

FROM $30 TO $40

- Dampierre Brut des Ambassadeurs Cuvée
- Duval-Leroy Brut NV
- Gosset NV Brut Excellence
- Henriot Souverain Brut Champagne
- Moët et Chandon Imperial (formerly White Star, it's the best-selling champagne in the United States)
- Nicolas Feuillatte NV Blue Label Brut
- Perrier-Jouet Brut
- Tarlant Brut Zero

FROM $40 TO $50 PLUS

- Billecart-Salmon Brut Reserve
- Bollinger NV Brut Special Cuvée
- Fleury Carte Rouge Brut Champagne
- Philipponnat Brut Royale Reserve NV
- Taittinger NV Brut La Française
- Veuve Clicquot Brut Yellow Label

RESOURCES

Here's where to find all the special tools, spirits, spices, and other ingredients mentioned in the book.

Introduction
9 Tiffany & Co. bubbles bracelet, www.tiffany.com

The Classics
14 Superfine tea strainer from Sur La Table, 800-243-0852 or www.surlatable.com

18 Les Parisiennes Morello cherries in brandy from the Gourmet Store, www.amazon.com

18 Angostura orange bitters, www.amazon.com

25 Rösle zester from Sur La Table, 800-243-0852 or www.surlatable.com

28 Beechwood muddler from Sur La Table, 800-243-0852 or www.surlatable.com

Bubbletinis
28 Madhava organic agave nectar (light) from Wild Organics, 888-598-8008 or www.wildorganics.com

31 Fee Brothers Bitters in orange and peach from Fee Brothers, 800-961-FEES or www.feebrothers.com; Angostura orange bitters, www.amazon.com

32 D'Arbo white elderflower syrup from German Deli, 877-GERMANY or www.germandeli.com

32 Star fruit (carambola) from Melissa's World Variety Produce, 800-588-0151 or www.melissas.com

Fruitful Fizz
36 Zipang sparkling sake from Liquorama, 877-981-9044 or www.liquorama.com

36 Lychee fruit from Yollie's Oriental Market, 317-780-8494 or www.yollie oriental.com

40 Torani passion fruit syrup from BevMo, 877-772-3866 or www.bevmo.com

Rose-Colored Glasses
46 Banfi Rosa Regale Brachetto d'Acqui, www.wine.com

51 Sour cherry syrup from Marco Polo, www.amazon.com

51 Les Parisiennes Morello cherries in brandy from the Gourmet Store, www.amazon.com

51 Torani pink grapefruit syrup from BevMo, 877-772-3866 or www.bevmo.com

Latin Libations
54 Hibiscus tea from www.iherb.com

57 Angostura orange bitters, www.amazon .com

57 Star fruit (carambola) from Melissa's World Variety Produce, 800-588-0151 or www.melissas.com

58 Passion fruit juice from Ipanema Girl, 718-545-2277 or www.ipanemagirl.net

61 Rhum Clément VSOP from BevMo, 877-772-3866 or www.bevmo.com

61 Fee Brothers orange bitters from www.amazon.com

Bubbles in Bloom
64 Monin violet syrup from Monin, 800-966-5225 or www.moninstore.com

64 Candied violets from Market Hall Foods, 888-952-4005 or www.markethallfoods.com

64 Monin jasmine syrup from Monin, 800-966-5225 or www.moninstore.com

67 Zhena's Gypsy Tea Red Lavender from Zhena's Gypsy Tea, 800-448-0803 or www.gypsytea.com

67 French dried lavender flowers from Herbalcom.com, 888-649-3931 or www.herbalcom.com

68 Pink dried rose petals from Herbalcom.com, 888-649-3931 or www.herbalcom.com

68 D'Arbo white elderflower syrup from German Deli, 877-GERMANY or www.germandeli.com

71 Madhava organic agave nectar (light) from Wild Organics, 888-598-8008 or www.wildorganics.com

77 Zipang sparkling sake from Liquorama, 877-981-9044 or www.liquorama.com

78 Madhava organic agave nectar (light) from Wild Organics, 888-598-8008 or www.wildorganics.com

Mixed and Muddled
78 Candied ginger from Market Hall Foods, 888-952-4005 or www.markethall foods.com

Happy Endings
84 Frozen Popsicle mold from Sur La Table, 800-243-0852 or www.surlatable.com

87 Snow-cone machine from Hawaiian Shaved Ice, 800-742-8334 or www.hawaiianshavedice.com

88 Monin lychee syrup from Monin, 800-966-5225 or www.moninstore.com

91 Torani pink grapefruit syrup from BevMo, 877-772-3866 or www.bevmo.com

92 D'Arbo white elderflower syrup from German Deli, 877-GERMANY or www.germandeli.com

ACKNOWLEDGMENTS

First I have to thank late California sparkling wine pioneer Jamie Davies for putting me onto the idea that bubbly is just wine beneath the bubbles and a great accompaniment to everyday life. And second, my first and best wine teacher, Karen MacNeil, for inspiring me to explore the mysteries of wine and to believe that I could help people unravel them.

This book would not have happened without my extraordinary agent Jennifer de la Fuente— a Bubbly Girl, coach, and friend; and Frank Scatoni of Venture Literary, who got it. I'll be forever grateful to my first Clarkson Potter editor, Amy Pierpont, for loving the idea of a book on bubbly and to succeeding editors, Judy Pray and Rosy Ngo, for helping make my final book sparkle.

Photographer Paul Body was a dream, always patient and creative with an unfailing sense of humor. Thanks to Harry, Patricia, and Haley Tweedie; Michele Joyce, and Pascal Courtin for letting me use their respective homes as photo studios.

A toast to Gillian Flynn and Brad Johnson of Modern Luxury for letting me write about what I love in their gorgeous magazines and Jayne McClinton and Phyllis Schwartz of NBC 7/39 San Diego for bringing "The Bubbly Girl" to television.

I so appreciate all my friends in the business who helped along the way and were always ready for a glass of bubbly: John Scharffenberger, Joy Sterling, Cate Conniff, Holly Peterson Mondavi, Suvir Saran, Ellen Flora, Robin Insley, Barbara Beltaire, Sami and Sharon Ladeki, Steve Pelzer, Jaime Rubin, Steve Goldberg, Jesse Rodriguez, Brian Donegan, Ellen Burns Van Slyke, Anne Stephany, Marguarite Clark, Nathaniel Christian, and Antonia Allegra. And bless Tom Mastricola and other brilliant bartenders around the country who let me watch.

Biggest thanks to the Hunt-Simpson family for making me the woman I am and to my adopted family of friends: Jerry McCormick, Mark Berry, Rob Akins, Jennifer Balanay, Wendy Downing, Sarah Robertson, Isabel Cruz, Kalisa and Don Wells, Kathryn Balint, Jane Clifford, Robin Stark, Boyd Smith, Lynette Holloway, Pia Tripline, Tim Klepeis, and the entire Coulon clan for all their encouragement. I hope this book will give you many more ways to celebrate the joys of life.